The ABCs
of a Good Teacher

Sharon P. Charles

TEACH Services, Inc.
P U B L I S H I N G
www.TEACHServices.com • (800) 367-1844

Copyright © 2015 TEACH Services, Inc.
ISBN-13: 978-1-4796-0508-8 (Paperback)
ISBN-13: 978-1-4796-0509-5 (ePub)
ISBN-13: 978-1-4796-0510-1 (Mobi)
Library of Congress Control Number: 2015909267

Published by

TEACH Services, Inc.
P U B L I S H I N G
www.TEACHServices.com • (800) 367-1844

Contents

Meet the Author..5

Dedication..6

Preface..7

Introduction...9

Ask pertinent questions...12

Believe every child has the potential to learn.....................13

Create a classroom atmosphere that is conducive to learning....14

Develop a good rapport with your students.........................15

Engage students in meaningful and
   enjoyable learning activities...16

Formulate clear goals and objectives 17

Give thoughtful suggestions and feedback 18

Help students when they encounter difficulties 19

Individualize instruction when necessary...........................20

Join a professional organization 21

Keep good records 22

Listen carefully when students share their thoughts,
   opinions, and ideas...23

Model the type of behavior you expect of your students...........24

Note details..25

Observe progress..26

Praise students' efforts..27

Question inappropriate behavior.......................................28

Respect your students..29

Seek opportunities for professional development 30

Take time to know your students 31

Understand individual differences in students.....................32

Verify information before drawing conclusions 33

Work diligently to accomplish your tasks...........................34

eXperience the joy of teaching 35

Yearn for success...36

Zoom to do an outstanding job..37

Meet the Author

Dr. Sharon Charles is an accomplished educator with over thirty years of experience. She spent more than twenty years at the Lew Muckle Elementary School, where she worked at a variety of positions, including coordinator of the schoolwide enrichment model program, teacher of gifted and talented students, reading coach, reading interventionist, and common core trainer.

She earned a bachelor's degree in elementary education and a graduate degree in teaching with a concentration in reading from the University of the Virgin Islands. She went on to earn a doctorate degree in instructional leadership from Argosy University in 2012.

She currently serves as part-time faculty in the College of Liberal Arts and Social Sciences at the University of the Virgin Islands, St. Croix Campus. She is the co-director of the Virgin Islands Writing Project and a member of the National Council of the Teachers of English, International Literacy Association, and the Association for Supervision and Curriculum Development. She has served in many executive positions including president of the St. Croix Council of the International Literacy Association. She is also a contributing author of the book *Voices From Behind the Scenes: Teachers Experiences in the Classroom Expressed through Poetry and Prose*.

Dedication

This work is dedicated to my mom and dad,
David and Muriel Charles,
who knew from the very start
that I wanted to be a teacher.

Preface

Dear Teachers,

I pray you had a rewarding summer experience filled with pleasurable moments spent with friends and loved ones. I extend warm greetings to you as you embark upon an unforgettable journey into a new school year. On a consistent basis, you sacrifice your time and resources to ensure that your students' needs are met. Although you are undercompensated for the work you do, you continue to represent your profession with pride and dignity. I thank you for your commitment to providing high quality education to students so they can be fully prepared for college and the workplace.

As the year unveils the multiple layers of roles you will be called upon to play, please remember that you are not alone on this journey. You share vital space with a group of educators who are passionate about enriching the lives of students. Reach out to your fellow educators for support. Exchange ideas. Capitalize on all opportunities to grow professionally so that you can enhance your knowledge and skills. Again, I thank you for accompanying me on this journey and for accepting the challenge to make a positive difference in the lives of our students. Please accept my best wishes for an enjoyable and rewarding school year.

Yours in education,

Sharon P. Charles, Ed.D.

Dear Students,

I am pleased that I have an opportunity to share my expertise with you. I know you may be experiencing a few uncertainties at this time, but I want you to develop confidence in yourself. In this class you have many rights, privileges, and responsibilities. You have the right to an excellent education. You have the privilege to express your ideas in a thoughtful and respectful manner. You have the responsibility to ask for clarification on anything you may be having difficulty with. It is my responsibility to ensure that you maximize your potential.

You must be busy wondering what we will be doing together for the next few months, but I can assure you that we will be working hard toward reaching our goals. Although I have a few goals for you while you are a student in my class, the ultimate goal is for you to develop a passion for reading and writing and expand your thinking and learning in all subject areas. I want to challenge your thinking and motivate you to study with diligence. I pledge to facilitate the learning process for you.

Please know that I have very high expectations of you. I respect your thoughts, ideas, and opinions, and I request that you do the same to me. We will collaborate on many issues that will impact your academic development. I take this opportunity to welcome you to my class, and I wish you a healthy and most rewarding school year.

Your teacher,

Sharon P. Charles, Ed.D.

Introduction

You book your flight to your favorite vacation destination. Coincidentally, the agent you spoke to was a student you taught in kindergarten. As you board the aircraft, you realize that the young man in the pilot's seat is one of your former first grade students. You take your seat, and as the aircraft soars into the air, you strike up a conversation with the passenger sitting next to you. Suddenly you both realize you share some commonalities. You were her second grade teacher. She is now a prominent attorney in one of the nation's biggest cities.

A deep feeling of pride descends on you. You have touched the lives of these students, and they have matured into the fruit of success. What a joyful feeling! Undeniably, teachers touch the future.

The ABCs of a Good Teacher

✓ Ask

pertinent questions.

Questioning is the gateway to discovery. A teacher's questions help to diagnose students' strengths and weaknesses. Teachers who ask good questions can gain insight into students' thought processes. Good questions can motivate students to delve into their imaginative spaces, explore the unknown, and find creative ways to solve problems. For best results, teachers should ask a variety of questions. Also, they should encourage students to formulate their own questions and compose responses to these questions. This not only provides students with practice, but it can help them to assess their learning. Questioning is one of the most potent tools that teachers have at their disposal.

✓ **Believe**
every child has the potential to learn.

Teachers who believe in their students exercise faith on a daily basis. They demonstrate patience, humility, and kindness toward their students. When teachers believe that all students have the potential to learn, they take time to understand their students' unique interests and abilities and provide them with the best learning experiences. When students know that their teachers believe in them, they strive to live up to their teachers' expectations.

✓ Create

a classroom atmosphere that is conducive to learning.

Classrooms should be so inviting that from the moment students arrive at the door they feel compelled to step inside. Within the walls of the classroom, furniture should be appropriately arranged and the room feature a rich display of the students' work. In this setting, students are encouraged to collaborate with each other and show appreciation for each other's efforts. The teacher facilitates students' learning, helping them to become critical thinkers, good decision makers, and problem solvers. Students in these classrooms are not afraid to share their ideas and opinions. Lessons in these classrooms are so engaging that students' motivation for learning is at a very high level.

✓ **Develop**

a good rapport with your students.

Teachers touch the lives of students every day. They can impact students negatively or positively by their action or inaction. Relationships built on honesty, respect, and trust can have long-lasting effects on teachers and students. When students discover evidence that shows teachers care, they are inclined to give their best effort. Building an excellent rapport with students is one of the most important things teachers can do in this profession.

✓ **Engage**

students in meaningful and enjoyable learning activities.

With careful planning, teachers can design lessons that not only challenge students' thinking but keep students engaged in their learning. If activities are enjoyable, students' interest and motivation will be high.

✓ **Formulate**

clear goals and objectives.

Goals are like a roadmap. They give directions to the place you would like to go. When teachers formulate clear goals, they are laying the foundation for effective instruction. When goals are clear, students know what is expected of them. Without clear goals, there is uncertainty, misunderstanding, and chaos. Teachers can ill afford these elements to invade the stability of their class-rooms. Even though the pathways to accomplishing specific goals may be different, each focused route will be traveled with courage and optimism.

✓ **Give**

thoughtful suggestions and feedback.

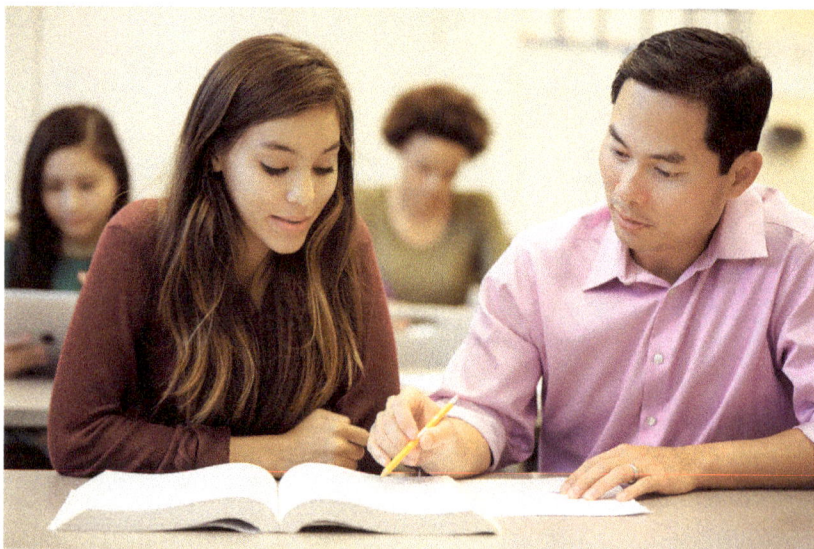

Feedback is an essential component in the learning process. Whether oral or written, feedback provides the opportunity for students to sustain their practice or make modifications for improvement. Students look to their teachers for critical feedback on their work. When teachers give thoughtful suggestions accompanied by specific directions, students are more inclined to respond positively. Fair, honest feedback goes a long way in helping students rise to excellence.

✓ **Help**
students when they encounter difficulties.

Adults and students encounter difficulties from time to time. The reasons for such difficulty vary, but the frustration that accompanies difficulty is sometimes unforgiving. When students encounter difficulty, the teacher should spend some time investigating the source of the difficulty and work with students to find solutions to the challenge. Effective teachers understand that some issues require the expertise of others. Teachers can make recommendations for additional assistance or ask for assistance. Collaboration among students is critical, as it helps them develop a level of trust that makes it easier to discuss conflicts and resolutions.

✓ **Individualize**
instruction when necessary.

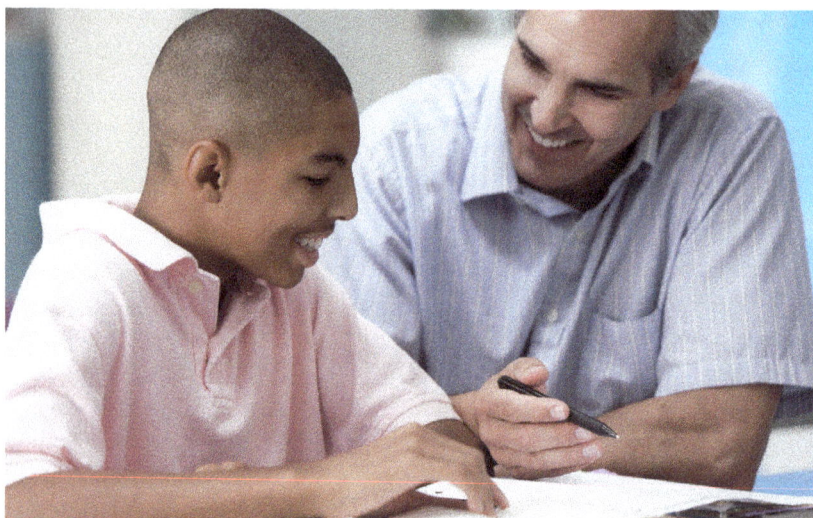

Even with the best made plans, teachers sometimes encounter situations where lessons have to be modified during the instructional phase. Such modification requires quick thinking and prompt decision making. The teacher may opt to re-teach the lesson, have students work with another student, work in a small group setting, or individualize the students' instruction. In the individualized instructional setting, the teacher works with one student at a time. Such interaction between the teacher and student allows for careful diagnosis of the problem and prescribing the appropriate intervention. Individualized work can also send a potent message to students that teachers care about their challenges and want to see them triumph over them. Such efforts can help to increase students' confidence and lead to greater academic outcomes.

✓ **Join**
a professional organization.

What better way can teachers enhance their learning than through collaboration that comes with membership in a professional organization? These organizations have established programs, and provide their membership with information through print and electronic media. Membership in professional organizations brings additional benefits including reduced rates for members to attend conferences and discounts on some resources. Knowing that you share the primary goals and vision of a professional organization can help to boost your self-esteem.

✓ **Keep**

good records.

Among the many tasks that teachers are required to do is one that requires them to keep accurate records. Data from classroom and standardized tests provide information on students' performance. Records provide support for critical actions and are the basis for the establishment of academic goals and plans for students' achievement. Many instructional decisions are based on records; therefore, it is important for teachers to maintain good records.

✓ **Listen**

carefully when students share their thoughts, opinions, and ideas.

If we were to stand at a corner and watch young children at play, we would quickly realize the wealth of ideas and opinions they possess. Teachers need to capitalize on students' enthusiasm and build time into their busy day to engage them in conversation about the concepts they are learning or topics that are of interest to them. Students who have developed the courage to share need to know that the teacher is paying attention to what is said. When teachers actively listen to students when they share their thoughts, opinions, and ideas, it sends a strong message that the teacher values their input.

✓ Model

the type of behavior you expect of your students.

What conflicting messages we sometimes send when our actions are not in harmony with our words! Whether in speech or action, students take pride in emulating the adults in their environment. When teachers model the type of behavior they expect of their students, this paves the way for a harmonious relationship.

✓ **Note**
details.

As a teacher, you have to be observant. Being observant puts you on track to thwart inappropriate behaviors. Teachers who pay attention to details are better able to articulate concerns over changes in students' attitudes and performance. Such notation can help teachers determine appropriate placement of students in programs for remediation or enrichment. When teachers note details, they have more information to make good decisions.

✓ **Observe**

progress.

Monitoring students' progress is an important part of teachers' responsibility. This provides critical information that will help teachers determine whether changes need to be made to instructional strategies, materials, or activities. Teachers can also evaluate students to determine which groups may need remediation or enrichment.

✓ **Praise**
students' efforts.

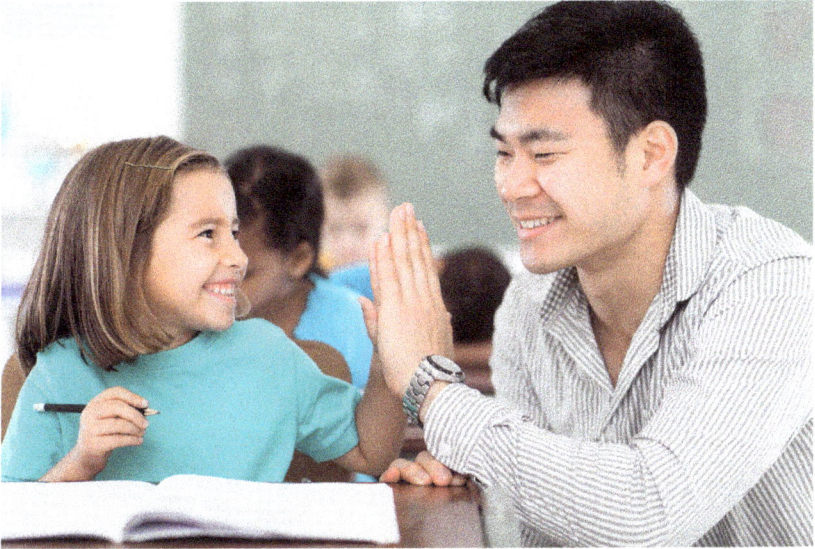

In any classroom setting, there will be students who are high achievers, average achievers, and low achievers. There will be students who are prepared to undertake the challenge and others who are reluctant to do so. Although all students do not perform at the same level, teachers should always praise students' efforts. Praise encourages students to strive for greater success. Praise motivates students to set their personal goals and work hard to achieve them. When teachers praise students' efforts, this brings positive results.

✓ **Question**
inappropriate behavior.

Effective teachers not only monitor students' academic progress, but they pay close attention to other aspects of students' lives that can have an impact on their achievement. Teachers need to observe students closely to ensure they are adhering to the rules that govern their behavior. Negative behavior distracts students from their work and impacts classroom routine. Once teachers observe inappropriate behavior, they need to intervene. Left unchecked, inappropriate behavior can prevent teachers from delivering instruction, alienate classmates, and create chaos in the classroom.

✓ **Respect**
your students.

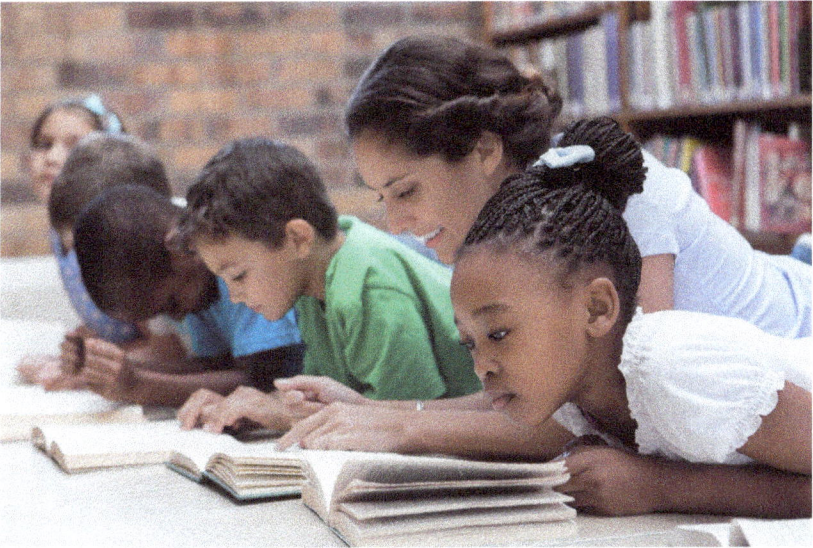

In order to gain students' respect, teachers should first show respect. If teachers demonstrate respect for their students, there would be fewer disciplinary problems in the classroom. When teachers respect their students, they set the foundation for the development of strong relationships. Students are more cooperative and willing to undertake challenges when there is mutual respect.

✓ **Seek**

opportunities for professional development.

The world of education is changing. Many of these changes will not only impact how students learn, but they will influence how teachers teach. To keep abreast of current trends in education, as well as issues that impact student achievement, it is incumbent on teachers to seek opportunities for professional enrichment. In order to grow in their profession, it is necessary that teachers view themselves as learners too.

✓ Take
time to know
your students.

Knowing your students spans far beyond all the "getting to know you" activities often conducted during the first week of school. Teachers need to take the time to diagnose students' strengths and weaknesses so that they can select appropriate intervention lessons and instructional practices that best cater to students' needs. Teachers should take time to listen, observe, and evaluate their students. They must be willing to utilize multiple sources of data to draw conclusions. Teachers should maintain contact with parents and guardians and continuously advocate for students. In addition, teachers should understand the social dynamics that impact students' learning. Knowing students also mandates that teachers gather information about students' interests and learning styles.

✓Understand

individual differences in students.

Students come to the classroom from different backgrounds. Consequently, they bring with them many varied experiences. Coupled with diverse interests, abilities, and learning styles, teachers have the gargantuan task of deciphering differences among students in order to bring the magic of teaching and the gift of learning to them. When teachers are equipped with background knowledge about student differences, the task of instructing students becomes less challenging.

✓ Verify

information before drawing conclusions.

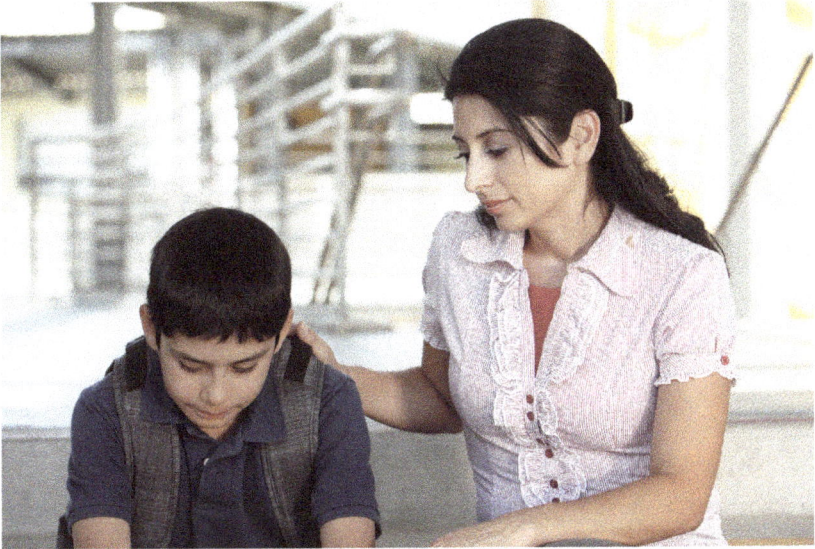

On a typical day, many events will capture teachers' attention. Before drawing conclusions, teachers need to ensure there is sufficient evidence to support their decisions. This will help to protect their integrity and win the respect of students, parents, and fellow educators.

✓ **Work**
diligently to accomplish your tasks.

Administrators, teachers, support staff, and parents play a vital role in the educational outcomes of students. These stakeholders bring diverse perspectives to the educational arena. Because of the multitude of tasks teachers are expected to complete on their instructional journey, it is imperative that they set clear goals and hold high expectations of their students. Organizing tasks into small, measurable steps will help to keep teachers on track as they work diligently to accomplish their goals.

✓ e**X**perience
the joy of teaching.

Teaching is a wonderful profession. It is one that allows you to nurture your passion, pamper your growth, and crown your success. As a teacher, you nurture minds, build bridges, make connections, and establish relationships for a lifetime. With your knowledge and guidance, you invite students to explore the world of opportunity. You not only prepare students for success at school, but you work diligently preparing them for success in their chosen careers. One of the greatest rewards as a teacher is to realize that you have done an exceptional job of equipping your students with the tools that will propel them into a successful future.

✓ **Yearn**
for success.

As a teacher, you invest in quality education for your students. Having formulated clear goals and objectives, you implement sound instructional practices that guarantee outstanding results. You collaborate with your students, giving them opportunities to share their ideas and opinions. You value their input. Your students are excited about learning, and you are passionate about teaching. Your students are on a journey to accomplishing greatness.

✓ **Zoom**
to do an outstanding job.

Teaching is not for the faint hearted. It is for the bold educator of children who is committed to nurturing young minds so that they can blossom into agents of change. Teachers not only impart knowledge, but they participate in the learning process as well. They invest in their professional development so that they can enhance their pedagogical skills, gain more content knowledge, and ultimately have a positive impact on students' achievement. Teachers know that the world is depending on them to produce competent citizens. Heartfelt gratitude is extended to all the teachers whose daily priority is to zoom to do an outstanding job.

What Teachers Do for Children

Teachers do a lot for children.
We encourage students to face the future with optimism.
With outstretched *arms*, we embrace them,
Shielding their fears, eliminating their anxieties,
And providing comfort in times of turmoil.
With our *heads*, we nod in acknowledgement of their bravery
And give our approval or disapproval for their words or actions.
With our *fingers*, we point them in the right direction,
Confident they will stay on the path that leads to success.
With our *eyes*, we search their minds for clues
That will provide answers to the mysteries that remain unsolved.
With our *eyes*, we help students to see that possibilities can be
    transformed into realization.
With our *ears*, we listen to their triumphs, challenges, and concerns.
With our *tongue*, we speak kind words.
With our *shoulders*, we provide a place for them to lean on
When they become overwhelmed with emotion.
With our *nose*, we teach them to smell the fragrance of the best
    gifts of life
And cherish them for a lifetime.
With our *brain*, we motivate them to be critical thinkers, decision
    makers, and problem solvers,
Willing to undertake the challenge to improve the quality of life
    for all in the community.
With our *feet*, we journey through the rough terrain,
Climbing mountains and descending steep cliffs,
Helping them to understand
That in their quest to achieve greatness
They must first attain the knowledge and skills
That will prepare them for the future.
As teachers, we do a lot for children.
We encourage them to face the future with optimism.

We invite you to view the complete
selection of titles we publish at:

www.TEACHServices.com

Scan with your mobile
device to go directly
to our website.

Please write or email us your praises, reactions, or
thoughts about this or any other book we publish at:

TEACH Services, Inc.
P U B L I S H I N G
www.TEACHServices.com • (800) 367-1844

P.O. Box 954
Ringgold, GA 30736

info@TEACHServices.com

TEACH Services, Inc., titles may be purchased in bulk for
educational, business, fund-raising, or sales promotional use.
For information, please e-mail:

BulkSales@TEACHServices.com

Finally, if you are interested in seeing
your own book in print, please contact us at

publishing@TEACHServices.com

We would be happy to review your manuscript for free.

www.ingramcontent.com/pod-product-compliance
Lightning Source LLC
Chambersburg PA
CBHW051213090426
42742CB00021B/3443